Business Recovery Planning

in a week

JACQUELINE CHAPMAN

Hodder & Stoughton

A MEMBER OF THE HODDER HEADLINE GROUP

Orders: please contact Bookpoint Ltd, 130 Milton Park, Abingdon, Oxon
OX14 4SB.
Telephone: (44) 01235 827720. Fax: (44) 01235 400454. Lines are open from
9.00–6.00, Monday to Saturday, with a 24 hour message answering service.
Email address: orders@bookpoint.co.uk

British Library Cataloguing in Publication Data
A catalogue record for this title is available from The British Library

ISBN 0 340 80493 9

First published   2002
Impression number   10 9 8 7 6 5 4 3 2 1
Year   2007 2006 2005 2004 2003 2002

Typeset by SX Composing DTP, Rayleigh, Essex.
Printed in Great Britain for Hodder & Stoughton Educational, a division of
Hodder Headline Plc, 338 Euston Road, London NW1 3BH by
Cox & Wyman Ltd, Reading, Berkshire.

The leading organisation for professional management

As the champion of management, the Chartered Management Institute shapes and supports the managers of tomorrow. By sharing intelligent insights and setting standards in management development, the Institute helps to deliver results in a dynamic world.

Setting and raising standards

The Institute is a nationally accredited organisation, responsible for setting standards in management and recognising excellence through the award of professional qualifications.

Encouraging development, improving performance

The Institute has a vast range of development programmes, qualifications, information resources and career guidance to help managers and their organisations meet new challenges in a fast-changing environment.

Shaping opinion

With in-depth research and regular policy surveys of its 91,000 individual members and 520 corporate members, the Chartered Management Institute has a deep understanding of the key issues. Its view is informed, intelligent and respected.

For more information call 01536 204222 or visit www.managers.org.uk

CONTENTS

■ I N T R O D U C T I O N ■

Business recovery planning, business continuity planning or disaster recovery. Whatever title you use, it is a necessity for every business ranging from one person working in the spare bedroom to the global conglomerate with sites everywhere.

This book is aimed at the smaller business, although it should provoke thought for the managers of larger ones. The aim is to alert you to the things you should think about, *before* you have to rescue your business from misfortune. No apology is made for thinking of the small business before the larger-scale needs of the corporate model – if you work in a large organisation the principles are the same, but the task is much bigger.

This book is a guide. All businesses have unique characteristics that only you can identify, yet all businesses have some degree of common ground where most of the work lies. You can use the advice given here to work out how to deal with the unique things in your business.

Business recovery planning is often neglected, presumably because nobody imagines they will need it. However, extremes of weather over the last few years have wrought havoc and brought structural damage and flooding to places that have not seen the like for centuries. Increasingly ferocious terrorist activity and the exploits of other activist groups have brought the very real threat of explosives and fire-bombs to many organisations and, in some cases, to individual employees of organisations.

Similarly, the acknowledged increase in crimes, such as burglary and car theft, can put the small business at risk. The loss of the home computer or laptop could mean the loss of all business data, particularly if there is no backup. Ignoring the possibility of disaster is like putting your head in the sand.

A business recovery plan will give you a chance to survive
and to maintain control of your business if problems occur. A
recent Gartner report suggested that, of businesses that
suffered a disaster, 60 per cent of them cease trading within
three years.

Business recovery planning means looking at all of the things
that might happen, assessing the risk and preparing a plan of
action if any of those things do happen. The insurance policy
that replaces the items or property you have lost will not be
enough.

When problems occur you need to be able to act rationally
immediately. Unfortunately it is very hard to be rational if
you are watching the building containing your entire
livelihood burn down. You know that all your business
records, stock or precious designs are not stored anywhere
else. You will be asked to make instant decisions that may
have implications later, but without a plan you will not have

thought about this. A business recovery plan means that, in a crisis, you will know where to find precise instructions of what to do.

As one well-known disaster recovery specialist puts it, 'In a disaster, people are unlikely to read a book'. However, if you read this book in advance and prepare a plan, your business is more likely to survive.

In this book, Sunday helps you to determine why you need a business recovery plan. Monday advises you on how to assess your needs.

Tuesday and Wednesday are devoted to developing your plan. Thursday looks at the realities of handling a disaster. What to do and when, may be obvious for dealing with a fire, but what do you do if your office is a crime scene and sealed off for days? How do you make sure that the local paper does not write you off as 'ruined'? Friday looks at the issues of implementing a recovery plan and Saturday examines other aspects of business recovery, stressing the importance of keeping everything under review. It includes some useful names and addresses of specialist organisations who will help you if you decide that this is not a task to tackle on your own.

This book will not prepare your recovery plan for you and you can choose to employ someone else to help you. However, unless the people who actually work in your organisation are involved in building and maintaining it, the plan will not work no matter how good it is.

Why do you need a business recovery plan?

The first stage in developing a recovery plan is to understand why you need one. This chapter looks at understanding:

- What a business recovery plan is
- What a disaster is
- The main components of your business and the impact of disaster upon them
- Where your business may be most vulnerable
- What plans you have made so far

What is a business recovery plan?

The business recovery plan itself is usually a set of documents that maps out all of the activities that need to take place in the event of a disaster. The plan guides the reader on where to obtain appropriate information or help. All the key people within the business need to be aware of the plan, be familiar with its content and know how to access it. There should be several copies of it. At least one copy needs to be stored away from the business.

The plan should be kept up to date! It is a living document and only as good as the information held in it. A plan that is 3 years out of date may not be of much help.

A business recovery plan does not protect you from competition or market forces, but in preparing it you may become aware of how your business could benefit from a competitor's disaster or vice versa.

Do not be afraid to discuss your plan with other
organisations and managers. You may be surprised to
discover how many have done nothing in this area.
Discussion and exploration of ideas can only help you. You
do not have to go into detail or discuss commercially
sensitive information in order to have a lively debate about
what could happen and what you should do.

What is a disaster?

The dictionary definition of a disaster is, 'an occurrence that
causes great distress or destruction: a thing, project, etc. that
fails or has been ruined'.

We all imagine disaster to involve fire, flood, plane crash or
earthquake. Over the last 15 years I have seen or felt all of
these, luckily with no ill-effects, but each could have been

catastrophic.

For your business, a disaster is any event that causes a loss of income that prevents you from trading. Such a broad definition covers many different things. A business recovery plan seeks to identify all such events and to suggest a countermeasure that can be used, either as part of your day-to-day activity, or as a resource or activity to be accessed if the relevant event occurs.

The components of your business

Your business has a *product*. This may be a service that you provide, based on skills you have. It may be something that you make – widgets, designer clothes or home-made sweets. Whatever your product is, if you stop producing it you stop making money. The aim of your business recovery plan is to maintain delivery of your product.

Your business has *customers* – people who buy your product. Your customers may stop buying your product for many reasons, but if they stop buying it because it is no longer available, you have reduced your future income. Retrieving those lost customers will take time. Your plan should help you to communicate with those customers and retain their loyalty.

Your business relies on *services from others* – raw materials, electricity, accountants, bankers. Their disasters are your disasters and you need to make sure that your plan takes this into account.

Your business has *staff* even if it is only you and a friend. 'There's nowt so queer as folk.' How often have you discovered something about someone that you would never have thought possible? Trust in people is essential, but contracts and legal agreements will afford you some protection if you find that your trust is misplaced or if someone else tries to take advantage.

Your *place of business* is located somewhere – in your home, on the business park, in town or in a shop on the high street. Your plan will investigate alternatives if you lose your premises.

Your business has *competitors*. How would it affect them if your business was ruined? Could you use this knowledge to salvage something from the wreckage? If your competitor has a disaster, can you gain an advantage? He or she may do the same to you.

Your business may be *unique* or have some unique characteristic. Recognise what that quality is and make plans to conserve it.

For all of the components mentioned, there are many events that would be a disaster for your business. Consider the following in respect of your business:

- Bad publicity – it does not have to be accurate to damage you and lose you customers
- Your main supplier goes bankrupt
- You lose a key member of staff
- A former employee has a grudge
- Your neighbour's premises are declared hazardous (they produce chemicals)

If any of these things could happen to you, along with the more obvious disasters of accident, fire or flood and you have not yet considered how to respond to them, then you should start to prepare a business recovery plan. The thinking process alone may make a difference to how you will react.

An essential component of any business recovery plan is recognising when to put that plan into operation. In later chapters, handling the kinds of incidents that are universally recognised as disasters are dealt with. However, when should a business recovery plan be initiated under other circumstances? Such occurrences will be identified further on in this book.

Where are you vulnerable?

Whether you are just starting up or you have built your business up slowly over time, or you are a new manager of an existing business or business function, it is important to understand where your weak points lie. In the next chapter there will be a detailed check-list for you to use to assess risk and vulnerability to problems. To start the thinking process you should consider some 'what if?' scenarios.

'What if your best/only salesperson was run over by a bus?'

- How do you manage their clients while they recover?
- How do you make sure that sales do not decline dramatically?

'What if your premises are ram-raided and all the stock is stolen?'

- How do you get replacement stock quickly?
- Are you insured for this?
- Was it an inside job?
- What do you need to tell the police?

What if you lose all of your client files because your computer system fails?

- Do you have backups?
- Is there a paper system that contains all the information?
- Why did it fail?
- How long will it take to replace it all?
- How will the business function in the meantime?

Other 'what ifs?' have probably already occurred to you. While they are fresh in you mind, write them down. You may need a memory jog later.

What plans have you made so far?

Most people have given business recovery planning some thought, although they may not have realised it.

These are the plans that you probably have already, even if you had not considered them as part of a business recovery process:

- Fire drills
- Evacuation plans
- Information from your insurers about how to make claims, and exclusions from your policy

You may also have some or all of the following:
- Insurance policies
- Computer system backups and restoration routines
- Third-party providers of some services, such as networks
- Off-site storage for stock or finished goods

Start to look at what you already do that would contribute to a business recovery plan. When you start to build the overall plan, you will need to gather all of this information together, so go and find it. Blow the dust off the files and photocopy the notices on the walls. If none of these things apply to you so far, get yourself a notebook – you will need one.

Summary

These are the benefits of having a business recovery plan:

- The plan is proof that you have thought through the impact of threats, including major disasters. This may reduce some of your insurance premiums
- Organisations that assess risks and take steps to counter them are more likely to reassure investors that their money is safe. This applies to banks, venture capitalists, private shareholders or your dad.

All of them will recognise that you have put thought into your business
- A plan really does improve your chances of surviving a disaster

You should now recognise why you need to develop a business recovery plan and you should have started to think about your business and the impact of a disaster upon it. Tomorrow we will look at how you should assess the needs of your business.

Assessing your needs

Before you can build your plan, you need to think about risk
and take a hard look at your business. You need to know
what activities your company is involved in. You need to
identify the external threats to your business and where you
are weak in countering them. You also need to calculate the
cost of recovery. Sometimes it will be more realistic to say: if
this event happens we are finished, so how can we protect
ourselves financially? Again the chapter is divided into
sections:

- Risk management and the Turnbull Report
- Your business and its main functions
- What are the main threats?
- Assessing the weaknesses
- What is insured (and what is not)?
- Counting the cost

Risk management

The whole topic of risk management can fill a book by itself,
but it is useful to think about what it means. Essentially risk
management is a process that we all undertake, often
unconsciously, when we make choices in respect of actions
we plan to take. Probably the most common risk
management that we all understand is insuring a car. You
know what the car is worth in monetary terms (although
insurance companies will not necessarily agree with you).
You know what the car is worth in terms of convenience. You
know who is going to drive it.

The insurance company will present you with a number of insurance options each of which has a price attached. From this information you decide what level of cover to choose, based on what you can afford and the amount of risk you think you can take – this is risk management. Imagine that the car is not worth much. Your 19-year-old son will drive it and the fully comprehensive premium is almost as much as the car's value. So, you choose the third party, fire and theft option, knowing that if anything happens you will not be any worse off than if you had taken the fully comprehensive cover.

The Turnbull Report

The Turnbull Report is a government-sponsored initiative that gives guidelines on how companies should manage risk. In summary, the Turnbull Report makes the following main points:

- Companies should actively set up a system of risk management that ensures that management (owners and directors) have a holistic view of potential threats and how to counter them. This should include:

  1) Evaluation and monitoring of risk
  2) Probability of risk occurring
  3) Impact of risk if it occurs
  4) The business ability to avoid or reduce that impact
  5) Whether the cost of preventative action is justified

- Companies should not just consider financial risk, but operational risk, including:

1) Risks that inhibit the business's ability to operate effectively and profitably
2) Risks that damage the reputation or share price of the firm or the company's assets
3) Risks that put the company at risk from legal proceedings

- It is recommended that all companies should comply with these guidelines to protect their investors, stakeholders and employees from the risks inherent in each business

Business recovery planning is one of the functions generated by companies that actively manage risk as part of their strategic activity. It may often form part of the company plan.

Risk is something that each organisation may handle differently and there are companies that specialise in risk management. If your company has unique issues that require specialist handling you should consider discussing your risks with such an organisation.

- High – likely to happen
- Medium – even chances of happening
- Low – not likely to happen

The rest of this section will talk about risk in terms of:

You may prefer to calculate risk in terms of percentages. It does not matter how you describe your evaluation of risk, provided that your evaluation is realistic.

Your business and its main functions

To start the assessment process you need to map out what
your business does. You can list the functions in accordance
with the types of people you employ.

> Accounts department
> Sales
> Marketing
> Stores
> Design office
> Production

If your business is very small (or very large) you can use a

technique called mind mapping®. This involves writing down activities and functions in bubbles as they spring to mind and linking them together as appropriate. The advantage of this technique is that you can put your thoughts and ideas down as they occur and let the connections appear later when you look at what you have written. The following diagram illustrates a basic mind map® for a small business.

As you can see, ideas can flow randomly and it is possible to see where all the connections are. The mind map can be expanded upon throughout this process to help build a fuller picture. The following example shows how simple ideas can be expanded to cover more detailed points.

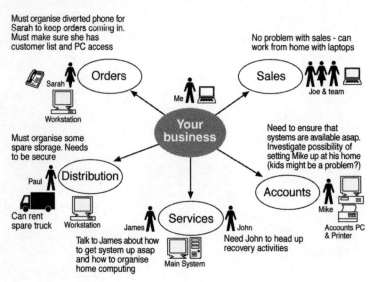

You may feel that you work better with pictures. If this is the case, take photographs of each area of your business. Take a team photo of all of the staff in a particular section, photograph key items of equipment or acquire pictures of that equipment from the manufacturer. Build a chart.

However you like to work, whether from lists, charts or diagrams, make sure it is clear to everyone who looks at it. Label pictures with names of equipment and people. Keeping it all in your head is not the right way to go about it.

What are the main threats?

The following table lists a number of events that can take place at any time. Using the table as a guide, look at your own business in relation to each event. Add others if appropriate and exclude those that do not apply. Calculate the risk of any of these happening to you in terms of high, medium or low.

Threat	Risk	Comments
Natural disaster – earthquake, etc.		Laughable but a recent tremor in the Midlands did cause minor structural damage to property. The UK is not immune, it just hasn't happened for centuries.
Fire on premises		Where are you vulnerable? Cables, storage areas, contractors working?
Fire on adjacent premises		What do they do? Are they higher risk?
Flood – burst pipes		Need to know if basements and roof spaces are vulnerable.

Threat	Risk	Comments
Flood – storm damage		Located on flood plain. Can storm drains cope?
Storm damage – structural		Hurricanes don't happen often.
Explosion – bomb		Animal rights. Anyone else?
Explosion – gas		Location of mains?
Accident		Flight paths, main roads, rail tracks.
Hostage-taking		Who and what impact?
Sabotage IT systems		Malicious staff or contractor activity.
Virus attack		Accidental or malicious?
Power failure		Strikes, cable damage, power station problems.
Loss of telephone services		Strikes, cable damage.
Theft		Stock, data, property.
Key staff		Death, illness, leaves to join a competitor, serious fraud.
Personal problems		Divorce, death of spouse.

Keep this table – you will use it tomorrow to plan how to counter high and medium threats.

Assessing the weaknesses

Using the previous list, take your mind map, list of functions or picture and think about the impact of threats to those functions. You can either develop another table or add to the mind map or picture. Additions to the mind map and table are illustrated below.

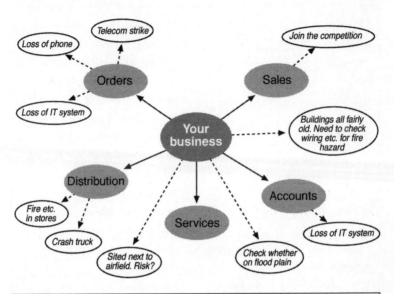

Threat	Risk	Departmental impact
Natural disaster – earthquake, etc.	Very low	Low risk but treat as major site disaster.
Fire on premises	Medium	Stores are most vulnerable. Major fire, treat as major site disaster.
Fire on adjacent premises	Low	Higher risk, but lots of space between buildings.
Flood – burst pipes	Low	Risk only apples to kitchen and toilets.
Flood – storm damage	Low	Flood plain (every 100 years). Stores most vulnerable. Use racking. Low-value items on bottom.
Storm damage – structural	Medium	Might lose roof. Check with structural engineer.

Threat	Risk	Departmental impact
Explosion – bomb	Low	No known reason for attack.
Explosion – gas	Low	No gas, but aviation fuel at airfield might cause blast damage. Evacuate building if fire at airfield.
Accident	Low	Parallel to landing strip. Commercial field, no training flights. Treat as major site disaster if it occurs.
Hostage-taking	Low	Seek advice but can't imagine why it would happen.
Sabotage IT systems	Medium	Check security on all IT systems.
Virus attack	High	Keep antivirus software up to date. Reinforce software policy.
Power failure	Low	Ensure IT can close down properly.
Loss of telephone services	Low	May cause problems if prolonged. Most orders are phone-based.
Theft	High	Keep client lists secure, make sure storage is kept locked at all times, fencing is maintained and alarms are set.
Key staff	Medium	Cross-train Sarah, Mike and James.
Personal problems	?	Don't know.

What is insured (and what is not)?

Before you go any further it is probably worth assessing what
insurance cover you have for the threats you have identified.
Take a copy of the table you have prepared or, for the mind
mappers, draw one up. Go through it, comparing it with
your insurance policies.

Threat	Insured?	Type of policy
Natural disaster – earthquake, etc.	Yes	Building and contents Consequential loss
Fire on premises	Yes	Building and contents Consequential loss
Fire on adjacent premises	? Check	Building and contents Consequential loss Compensation and claims against third parties
Flood – burst pipes	Yes	Building and contents Consequential loss Compensation and claims against third parties
Flood – storm damage	Yes	Building and contents Consequential loss
Storm damage – structural		Building and contents Consequential loss
Explosion – bomb	? Check	Building and contents Consequential loss Compensation and claims against third parties
Explosion – gas	Yes	Building and contents Consequential loss Compensation and claims against third parties

Threat	Insured?	Type of policy
Accident	Yes	Building and contents Consequential loss Compensation and claims against third parties
Hostage-taking		?
Sabotage IT systems	? Don't know	Consequential loss
Virus attack	? Don't know	Consequential loss
Power failure	No	
Loss of telephone services	No	
Theft	Yes	Building and contents Consequential loss
Key staff	? Check	Critical illness Life assurance
Personal problems	No	

If you cannot find your insurance documents or you have got any, you need to consider what to do next. A good insurance broker is the best source of advice in this respect. Find one you think you can trust – there is some information at the end of the book to help you.

Counting the cost

You must bear in mind that everything you do to ensure the security of your business has a cost. You must budget for that cost in the same way that you budget for other aspects of your business.

There are some essential costs that come with your business:

- Third party liability insurance
- Buildings and contents insurance
- Motor insurance

These are costs you almost certainly bear already.

Other types of insurance are available at a premium. You must weigh up whether that premium is too high for the risk involved.

If you occupy business premises you should have been visited by your local fire officer. He or she will have identified areas of risk and recommended or imposed the precautions you must take. The provision of appropriate equipment should also be included in your costs.

If your business is an office in your home, you may not have given this much thought. Smoke alarms are the minimum precaution anyone should take. However, if your business is your entire livelihood you should consider putting in a fire-proof safe (for those essential documents and computer disks) or identifying a remote site to store copies of these critical items.

Alternatives to your existing business arrangements in case of disaster, whether they are suppliers, equipment or buildings, all have a cost. You might get a bigger discount if you seek a sole supplier, but it is worth calculating the cost of having an alternative option. The loss of 1 or 2 per cent in discount may be less than having to pay premium prices when you have no other choice. Spare premises are probably too large a drain on resources but reciprocal arrangements with other businesses might not be. Equipment lying idle, albeit new, still depreciates. Find out the cost and availability of rental.

You may decide that the cost of protecting some aspects of the business is too high and that you prefer to live with the risk. There are insurance products that cover this option as well.

When you have decided what you can afford, you can take steps to counter the weaknesses you have identified. You are already strengthening your business because some of the threats are now reduced.

Summary

Monday has been spent taking a good look at your business.

You should now be aware of the following:

- What your business does
- The main threats to your business
- The weaknesses in your business
- The options available to counter those weaknesses
- What is insured and what is not

You should have prepared a series of charts or tables containing all this information. Put it somewhere safe and talk it over with a colleague or partner to make sure you haven't forgotten anything.

On Tuesday and Wednesday we will look at developing the plan itself.

Developing your plan I

The next two days will be spent putting together the plan.
Today we will look at:

- Key people
- Key systems
- Special needs of IT
- Practical preparation

Key people

Key people are usually those who bring something unique to
your organisation – it may be that you have a designer who
is extremely talented, a technician who can make anything
work or a salesperson who could sell ice to Eskimos. Look at

your people, decide how valuable they are and think about what you would have to do if they were not there. The following options may be applicable to your key people:

- Critical Employee Insurance will cover you if they are sick or die
- Employment contracts with extended notice periods (3–6 months) for those with specialist skills should allow you time to recruit a replacement
- Contract terms which include clauses to prevent your employee from working for a competitor or in your location for a set period of time.

More positive activities include:

- Reward key people appropriately for the skills they bring to your organisation
- Succession planning – who else could do what they do, where can you find design talent – local universities or colleges?

It will probably help to compile a table of your key staff. Keep the table up to date and keep a copy of it in your emergency pack and as part of your recovery plan. If you do not want this information to be known within your company, store it in a sealed envelope or as an encrypted file within your computer system (make sure you can get at it). Save it within your personnel records system, but make sure you know who your key employees are and why.

Key employees table		
Post details	**Post holder details**	**Protective actions**
• Role • Reason for being key employee	• Name • Address etc.	• Insurance • Extended notice period • Restrictive contracts
• Designer • Builds and improves specialist tools	• Mike Peters • The Big House The Street, Anytown	• Three months notice • All equipment patented in company name • Key employee insurance
• Sales Director • Holds details of all major clients	• John Smith • 1 The Roadway Anytown	• Three months notice • May not work for a competitor company for up to 12 months after leaving employment under any circumstances • Must not retain any company records in any format upon leaving the company

You will also need to know who is going to do what in an emergency and how to contact these people. They also need to know what to do but this is dealt with later in this chapter.

Keep contact lists simple but include *all* of the following information:

- Name
- Address
- Telephone number
- Mobile number – *are you sure this is up to date?*
- Car registration number – *who owns each car in the car park?*
- Department
- Extension number
- Next of kin details – *don't get this wrong!*
- Prime contact (in the event of disaster) Y/N
- Role – *a very brief description of what you want them to do*
- Key holder Y/N + details
- First aider Y/N
- Fire warden Y/N

There may be other information you wish to record against this list but do not overcomplicate it. Keep this list up to date. Make sure there is a copy in the emergency pack.

Key systems

Systems covers many generic functions. You should be able to determine what each system consists of and what it does. You have already looked at the main risks and whether that system is vulnerable. Identify which of these risks would seriously impact your main systems and measure those systems in terms of the risk. If you manufacture using flammable materials, the risk of fire is necessarily higher. You can assess the likelihood of that risk becoming a reality by looking at your levels of prevention. This will give you an opportunity to revise that risk level.

To evaluate the impact of a problem or risk, you need to look at the things your organisation does and decide whether failure in any one area would seriously affect your profitability. What do you rely on? Would it really matter if the accounts department stopped working for a few days? How about delivery of raw materials or stock – what have you done to ensure a continuity of supply? If your main production machine was damaged by vandals, could you get it working again before it cost your company too much?

Regulations and legislation – are you sure that you comply with any legislation that applies to your business? – Do not be forced to stop trading because you have failed to keep up to date. This is a sensitive area, particularly for small businesses that may be unable to afford modifications brought about by changes in legislation. If this sort of change might drive you out of business, you should consider discussing your options with your accountants and lawyers.

Again, it is useful to draw a table or another mind map. Identify all the business processes (you have done this once already on page 20). Assess the risk to each and the impact on the business if the worst happened to that system. How long can that system be out of operation? What is most important about the system? Who are the key staff involved and what have you put in place to counter the risks? The table below contains basic details. Your table should contain as much information as possible and you should cross-reference to other tables or lists. When you are away or abroad, representing your company, your staff have to be able to follow the plan.

System (e.g. department or activity)	Admin office & accounts	Design	Production	Stores – raw materials	Stores – finished goods	Distribution
Level of risk (how likely it is)	Low	Low	High	Medium	Low	Low
Impact (how big an effect will it have)	Medium	High	High	High		Low
Location (where the system is located)	Main building	Main building	Main building	Store 1	Store 2 Store 3	Main building & car park
Allowable outage (how long can you manage without it)	3 days	4 weeks	4 weeks	2 weeks	4 weeks	1 week
Business critical items (what data or machines critical to the business are within this system)	Clients lists/ Suppliers/ Accounts system/ Order and delivery schedules/ Personnel details	Design computers and prototyping tools	Specialist jigs	None	None	Van
Number of staff [key staff] (how many staff in the dept; how many are essential)	6 (2 key) See staff list	2 key	7 (1 key)	2	1	1
Insurable value (£) This information will be contained in your insurance policies	replacement	Insured at replacement value	Insured at cost value	Insured at cost	Insured at cost	
Contingency plan (what has been prepared already in case of disaster)	All data backed up remotely. Local office space available for easy rental, see list of essential suppliers	As Admin & accounts. Tools – 3-week lead time for delivery of replacement	Jigs insured Agreed build time for replacement is 2 weeks	JIT supplies+ emergency arrangement with suppliers	Split-site storage	Insured Rent van

Special needs of IT

Information Technology occupies a place in most organisations. For many, the IT system is the place where all the corporate data is stored. If you do not use computers at all, you can skip this section of the book. If you have any computer system, ranging from a stand-alone PC or laptop to a 5000 workstation area network, you should pay attention to this section.

Those with large systems and separate IT departments should have set up a disaster recovery plan in-house or with a specialist organisation. This will include any or all of the following options:

- Hot site with a mirror image of your systems that can be activated within hours of a major disaster
- Reciprocal arrangements with other sites within your company that enable your system to be hosted while repairs are carried out
- Off-site storage of backed up data and regular practices of restoring data
- A comprehensive backup strategy that ensures all critical data are backed up at least daily and stored safely away from the business premises
- Comprehensive system documentation that allows rapid redeployment of systems on a new site
- Key staff trained and able to move to an alternative site and begin recovery operations

If you are not sure how to go about this, contact a disaster recovery specialist company. There are several sites on the internet for disaster recovery specialists. They should be able to send you an information pack of what you need to do. Alternatively, discuss your options with your normal hardware, maintenance and software suppliers. Identify whether they can offer you any form of disaster recovery within the terms of support contracts that you may have with them.

For the smaller business (less than 50 staff and a single network) the following are essential:

- Off-site storage of backed up data and regular practices of restoring data
- A comprehensive backup strategy that ensures that all critical data are backed up at least daily and stored safely away from the business premises
- Comprehensive system documentation that allows rapid redeployment of systems on a new site

If you only have a single PC or laptop, you should still backup and practise restoring your data. You should keep a copy of what your system consists of and the software on it. Backup is easily carried out using either a CD-writer or backup tape drives, *but* you must carry out backups at regular intervals depending on how much data you input each day. You must also store the backup away from your place of business.

A detailed description of your system and what it consists of should be kept in your emergency pack, along with original or backup copies of your application software (Microsoft packages or similar, software written or designed exclusively for your organisation plus any other off-the-shelf software). This information will allow you to rebuild your system within a very short period of time usually only as long as it takes to buy the components from a supplier, connect them together and load the software and data.

Practical preparation

This section contains the most work because this is where the detail lies. The employees in your organisation have to be involved and contribute.

You have already prepared a table giving a broad outline of your key systems. You now need to go into much more detail. Once again, tables are probably the easiest way to record the information you need.

Site information looks at each area and records everything about it and what needs to be done during a disastrous event.

Disaster actions identifies what needs to happen to each element on the site to enable rapid recovery following a particular event.

Examples of the tables have been included in pages 39–40 with further detailed planning on pages 41–43. It is suggested that you draw up templates for the relevant staff to complete, so that the information is recorded in a consistent way.

You, however, have a rather different task to consider. If your entire site was destroyed you need to make two critical decisions. This is your disaster recovery policy – it represents a stake in the ground, beyond which you are not prepared to go.

1 Is it realistic to rebuild the business (for a large multi-
   site organisation this might not be necessary, for
   anyone else facing total destruction it is)?
2 If it is realistic, where do we work from, and in what
   order must we start again?

Finding an alternative site quickly may be difficult, but not impossible. It helps if you maintain a watching brief on the available sites in your location.

Starting again means prioritising your business functions putting resources into those things that need to continue regardless, but adding extra effort to those that need to be rebuilt.

Attach a site plan that includes a detailed layout for switches, valves and the location of critical equipment and emergency equipment. One copy is to be kept in the department and one copy in the emergency pack. A further copy should be kept in the admin office.

The plan will also include activities to be carried out after the event. Each page lists activities with the individual responsible for them. It may look something like this:

Disaster actions table

Recovery Team Leader: John Smith
Finance: A N Other
Production: A N Other
Sales team: A N Other
Design: A N Other

Stores: A N Other

Immediate Actions

- Recovery team to meet in Meeting Room 6, or if site destroyed, at Town Hotel, Main Street
- Bring departmental plan for recovery
- Confirm recovery priorities
- Arrange for all post to be diverted to PO box
- Set up telephone system in emergency office

After first meeting

- Arrange to visit injured staff or next of kin
- Contact own staff personally or using agreed cascade and advise them of immediate situation
- Call relevant numbers on support system list
- Contact rental agency for replacement equipment, quote contract no: nnnn, request delivery for dd/mm/yy
- Visit new offices and assess layout. Unpack recovery box supplies
- Advise suppliers of furniture and equipment details
- Update Team Leader
- Visit disaster site, arrange for retrieval of undamaged equipment if appropriate

At regular intervals

- Update staff
- Attend recovery meetings

As required

- Set up replacement equipment
- Call staff back to work
- Maintain record of activities and costs
- Identify additional losses and requirements
- Liaise with insurance assessors
- Work with investigators

Site information table

Department name: Manager name: Extension:		Location:	
Description of department function:		**Period department could be out of use before disruption to business ___days?**	**Recovery priority** High Medum Low
List staff	**Responsible for**	**Electricity**	**Water**
1	1	Cables Voltage	Pipes Valves
2	2		
3	3	Switchgear Fuses	Drains Tanks
4	4		
5	5		
6	6	**Gas** (mains or LPG)	**List high-risk substances**
7	7	Pipes Valves	1
8	8		2
9	9	Tanks	3
10	10		4
List critical equipment 1 2 3 4 5	**Replacement options** 1 2 3 4 5	**Specialist information**	

Emergency equipment and location
1 *This section identifies the location of specific*
2 *equipment including fire-fighting equipment*
3 *or specialised items for your environment*
4
5

Main actions in the event of a disaster *This section contains the main actions to be carried out in the event of a disaster on site, e.g. close fuel supply valves, shut fire doors, etc. The boxes below identify activities for specific types of disaster*

	Fire	Flood	Explosion	Accident	Theft	Other
Alarm	1	1	1	1	1	
Contact	2	2	2	2	2	
Gas	3	3	3	3	3	
Electricity	4	4	4	4	4	
Water	5	5	5	5	5	
Equipment	6	6	6	6	6	

Other information

The plan is described briefly here. When you build your own
it will contain much more detail on a departmental basis.

If you are a sole trader, your plan may be much more simple:

- Call all numbers on support system list
- Talk to insurers
- Visit alternative premises – this might be your spare
  bedroom
- Set up replacement equipment – this may mean
  visiting your local store to buy new tools (keep the
  receipts) or calling the supplier to see when your
  new make of widget can be delivered
- Reload software and data from backup disks
- Discuss event with fire and/or police officers

No matter how large or small your business even the outline plan of the steps you need to take will help you to decide what needs doing.

Summary

You have now completed most of the information-gathering that you need to do before compiling your plan. On Wednesday you will collect up the last pieces of information and put the plan together.

Developing your plan II

Today we will finish collecting information and compile the plan.

- Support systems
- The emergency pack
- Compiling your plan
- Communication
- Updates

Support Systems

These are the people you will need to contact in the event of a disaster. Once again an up-to-date list or table will be essential. These suppliers will need to be notified for one or all of the following reasons:

- Making safe
- Terminating or reconnecting supplies
- Initiating claims
- Initiating disaster plans
- Courtesy
- Accuracy of information
- Accessing funds
- Security
- Investigations

Each supplier will have specific information requirements and these should be recorded in the table. Copies of policies and agreements should be held securely, preferably at a remote site. At the least, account numbers or contract numbers should be recorded here as well as basic contact information. To construct your table, contact each of the relevant suppliers and check that the contact details are correct. Ask the supplier what information they will require in the event of a disaster. On the list, identify who in your organisation will make the initial contact to start recovery operations in motion. Make sure this information is also recorded in departmental plans. This table should be regularly updated.

Service	To be contacted by	Supplier name, address, telephone /fax number	Account number and contact details	Information required by supplier
Emergency services		999		
Police (local number)				
Fire (local number)				
Main services				
Telephone services				
Electricity supplier				
Gas supplier				
Water supplier				
Local council				
Business services				
Landlord				
Architect				
Accountants				
Lawyers				
Bankers				
Insurers				
Principal contractors				
Plumbing				
Cabling				
Heating				
Computer services				
Catering supplies				
Disaster contacts				
Coroner				
Structural engineer				
Insurance assessor				
Media				

There are a few suppliers who merit special mention in this
section.

Lawyers

Many small businesses do not employ a lawyer on a regular
basis – they tend to go to someone when they need help. This
is fine for most of the time, but you must know who to use.
Lawyers have special interests and it is more effective to find
the best in the field. If you do not have knowledge in this
area then it is very likely that your insurance company will. If
you are in dispute with your insurer speak to the Law Society
and ask for details of who can help you. Regardless of your
situation, it may be helpful for you to retain the services of a
legal firm to handle any routine things. You will then build a
relationship which may help you in the future.

Accountants

Amost all businesses employ accountants. Do discuss
business recovery planning with your accountant. They will
identify tax-effective ways of funding it and they will advise
you on the proportion of turnover/profit you should be
investing in it. They will also be able to handle the financial
aspects of managing a crisis if they have been involved in the
planning.

Insurers

You have to have insurance and your insurer is principally
interested in taking your premium and keeping it. Use a
good broker because this type of insurance is not sold
directly. Obtain several comparative premium quotes
because prices will vary from company to company as will
benefits. You need to make sure you have cover for the
following:

- Liability insurance in case of death or injury to staff or customers
- Premises insurance
- Stock insurance (raw materials and finished goods)

There are several other opportunities for insurance, including key staff insurance and specialised insurance for equipment, such as cranes or heavy plant. Whatever you choose to cover, make sure that payment will be made in the event of claims and that there are no onerous pre-conditions. Also, ensure that excesses are manageable.

Computer systems disaster recovery

If you business relies heavily on effective computer systems, you may employ the services of a disaster recovery specialist. In these circumstance you will have an ongoing relationship with this company which will include regular backup and recovery tests and often a full disaster recovery mobilisation. Only you can judge whether or not you need this degree of support. Like all other backup systems this has a cost.

The emergency pack

This is exactly what it says it is – in a small organisation it may simply be a briefcase containing a copy of the business recovery plan, a backup of the computer and a spare mobile phone. In a larger organisation it may consist of several packing crates stored off site but easily accessible. What is important is its contents. When a major disaster strikes,

emergency procedures usually dictate that you leave the premises and you do not return until it is safe. However, that might take several days and in the meantime your business is dying. The emergency pack provides you with the minimum you need to continue working.

The table below suggests a number of items that might be useful to have on hand when disaster strikes. It is utterly pointless keeping the box in the office. If you work from home ask a friend or nearby relative, to store the box for you. Alternatively, you may be able to make reciprocal arrangements with another small business – this can work in other ways as well. The key thing is to ensure that you can access this box within 30–60 minutes during working hours. If necessary have two identical boxes stored in different locations.

Practical items

These are things that might come in handy immediately after a disaster. It is not essential to include these items but it may save time and it will certainly save effort.

Item	Reason for inclusion	In/out
Torch with lots of spare batteries	Power is usually cut off and businesses often rely on lighting dark spaces – emergency power may not be appropriate.	
Rope	Securing things, using as a makeshift banister, a cordon. Sam Gamgee in *Lord of The Rings* knew the wisdom of having a strong piece of rope.	
Dust/Toxic fume masks	Dust is everywhere!	
Hard hat	You might find your own more comfortable than a borrowed one.	
Wellington boots	Water is depressingly familiar in many disasters.	
Strong chain and padlock	You may want to secure some items until such time as other support services arrive.	
First aid kit	Broken glass gets everywhere.	
Tools – hammer nails, screwdrivers, etc.	Always useful.	

Essential items

Those things without which you cannot even start to function.

Item	Reason for inclusion	In/out
Business recovery plan	It is your bible.	
Spare keys	You may need these to lock up undamaged rooms, and so on. The originals will almost	

	certainly have been left behind.	
Duplicate company seals, or any other item that is considered to be essential to the business but exists as a 'one off'	Having easy access to such items that you do not waste weeks waiting for a duplicate.	
Spare credit card (small businesses only)	A credit card account with a sensible limit will allow you to buy what you need. It will also contain all the costs you incur in one place which will make claiming from insurance easier. Finally, when cash is short you will not have to find so much money when starting to make repayments.	
Petty cash	You will need some, even if it is only to get cups of tea. In extreme circumstances you may be giving your employees enough cash to get home – if their handbags and wallets are currently being consumed by flames.	
Stationery	A small supply of headed paper, stapler, sellotape pens, folders, etc. will be useful .	
Computer backup, disks, tapes, etc.	You can almost certainly buy a new computer off the shelf with the relevant peripherals to reload your business systems. If you are a larger organisation you will be calling your service supplier. All of your data is on this media.	

| Mobile phone | This need only be a 'pay as you go', but make sure it has credit. If the worst comes to the worst, all of your business calls can be redirected to it and wherever you end up working, your calls will still come to you. | |
| Dictaphone | Use this to record all the things you need to do. It will save endless pieces of paper. | |

There may be many other items that you decide you need and the larger your organisation the longer this list will be. If you business is located in a remote area you may also want to arrange for the provision of temporary toilets and more other essential items. These do not belong in an emergency pack but they should be readily available.

Compiling your plan

By now you should have the following tables:

- Possible risks
- Employee details
- Key employees
- Key systems
- IT Systems
- Site details for each key system
- Support systems
- Practical and essential items for emergency boxes

You may have gaps in these tables where you do not have an answer. Fill the gaps. Some of the gaps may be to do with contingency plans that you do not have. You may realise that you need to arrange for someone to supply specific disaster recovery services. Or perhaps a specialist piece of equipment has no contingency plan attached to it. NOW is the time to make these arrangements. Only you can do this. If you have found an area where you are at significant risk you should address it as quickly as possible. Finding a gap should not stop you from continuing with the plan, but your plan will not be complete until you have filled all the gaps.

The following diagram illustrates how all the components of your plan fit together. Your plan will consist of all of these elements contained in one place. Implementation of your plan relies on the ability to distribute these elements to the relevant people in order for them to execute the plan.

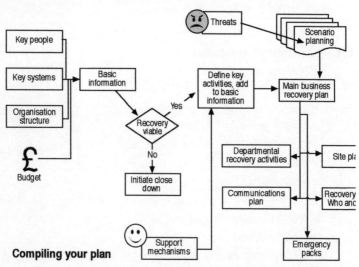

Compiling your plan

To give everyone in your organisation an idea of where to start, it may be useful to carry out some scenario planning and include these in your recovery plan. This consists of looking at particular events and constructing an action plan for each of them. The action plan will contain check-lists of activities to be carried out.

For example, a major supplier goes bankrupt, your check-list could look like this:

- How much stock do you have? Estimate when stock will run out
- How much is on order, will it be delivered? Confirm that this will happen and revise stock estimates if appropriate
- Does the company owe you any money or stock? Contact the receivers or administrators and advise them of your claim
- Is any additional stock available from the company or have they ceased trading altogether? If the receivers or administrators are continuing to sell stock and you have room to store it, make an offer – you may get it at a reduced price if cash is required
- How soon can your alternative supplier start to deliver? Contact your alternative supplier to ensure they have sufficient capacity to meet your requirements
- Who else can supply you? Look for another alternative supplier

A physical disaster such as fire or flood will necessitate a check-list with more steps in it, but will consist of the following main phases:

- Damage limitation – this includes activities such as evacuating buildings, raising the alarm or carrying out defensive actions, e.g. closing stopcocks or activating fire-defence systems like sprinklers or inert gas systems

- Damage assessment – this means identifying the damage done. Your site lists will be invaluable here. The support lists that enable you to contact the relevant organisations are extremely important too
- Recovery – all of your alternatives should come together to allow you to continue trading. Future sections of the book cover this

Communication

There is one list left to complete.

Put together a list of your customers. Basic details will be all you will need:

- Name
- Address
- Telephone number
- A brief summary of key information to be given to customer – emergency or temporary telephone numbers, etc.

You may also want some summary information about what they buy and date of their last order, although this information should be available on your computer system backups if you have one. It will be important for you to be able to tell your customers what has happened.

Your plan is now a folder full of lists and scenarios. Key people have been identified to carry out certain tasks but who knows exactly what to do? Ideally when you put your plan together, you will discuss it with all the relevant people.

However, if your organisation is very small, you may have compiled the plan yourself. Discuss the plan with your partners or staff. Review aspects of it with your insurance company, your local fire officer or police crime prevention officer. Test it! Make sure that everyone knows what part they have to play. You should carry out fire drills and practise other disaster scenarios, particularly if they are high risks for your business.

Can your business recovery plan help other businesses in the same building or industrial park? Are there opportunities for synergy? Talk to other businesses about ways that you can help each other, even if it is only reciprocal agreements for storing backup tapes for IT systems.

Updates

All the tables and charts you have used to develop your plan must be kept up to date. This cannot be emphasised often enough. To build a plan and then file it away is almost as bad as not making one at all. The emergency packs also have to be kept up to date. System backups, updated name and address lists should all be maintained as accurately as possible.

Maintaining the plan and all of its attendant documentation is a regular task for everyone involved in the plan. When people leave your organisation, make sure that their replacement is briefed and kept up to date with their responsibilities. If you add functions or departments, they too need to be included.

Summary

The plan is now as ready as you are able to make it. Tomorrow we will look at what happens when disaster strikes.

Handling a disaster – it's happening now!

After putting the plan together you need to think about how you would actually use it. Today we will go through all of the things that you will need to do if a disaster happens. If you choose to, you can include detailed instructions in your plan. Nevertheless, events have a habit of overtaking and there will not be time for revision – a check list should be enough to ensure that everything is done. Today we will cover:

- Identifying the disaster
- Calling emergency services
- Evacuation plans
- Essential contact management
- Media management

Identifying a disaster

In some instances disasters are obvious. If the building is blazing, it is a disaster and most of today will be spent looking at this type of event. There are, however, other events which, although much less dramatic, can be equally disastrous for your business. You know your business, you know where you are vulnerable and you should be aware of the tell-tale signs that trouble is brewing.

- If your IT systems are plagued by viruses then defend them – loss of IT systems and data can destroy a business as effectively as any fire
- Discovering that a trusted employee is stealing from

your company will be a shock, but if you have not put proper audit controls in place it may turn into a disaster. You could discover that you are being sued for the non-payment of bills and the money to pay them has been siphoned off into exotic holidays, has paid for the employee's new car or conservatory

* Failure to replace a faulty machine guard may cost you your business if someone is seriously injured and you are sued by the individual and/or the Department of Trade and Industry (DTI). Compensation payments can exceed any insurance you may carry

Do not be complacent! From a pragmatic point of view it is unrealistic to initiate full business recovery plans unless the event closes your business. For the most part, people tend to think that fire is the most likely event, but the following can also close you down:

* Major theft of stock – this should be a temporary set-back, but inconvenient. Send staff who cannot work home and allow the police and insurers to do their work. When supplies start to return to normal, allow staff to return to work
* Failure to comply with safety regulations – this is avoidable, but if a serious accident occurs then your premises may be closed until an investigation has been carried out. Send affected staff home. Negotiate to allow office staff to continue working. Ensure communications are regularly made to staff. Carry out immediate remedial action to allow staff to return to work. Cooperate with investigators

- Problems on other people's premises – if you are unable to access your premises because of a major problem on a neighbouring site, send your staff home until it is safe for them to return. Communicate with the crisis manager of the affected site. Make sure your own site is made safe and discuss how to do this with the emergency services on site. Call only essential staff in to do this. Initiate claims for loss of income, etc.
- Riots and subsequent damage – send staff home. Secure your premises as fully as possible. Liaise with police and other relevant services as appropriate
- Crime committed by others on your premises – send affected staff home and allow the police to complete their investigations. When investigations have finished, initiate cleaning or damage repair and recall staff to work. Seek compensation if appropriate
- Terrorist activity in your location – secure your premises and send staff home. Cooperate with the police to ensure the safety of all

Calling emergency services

It may seem like stating the obvious: 'The building is on fire, call the fire brigade!', but when confronted with making a 999 call many people struggle to remember essential information. They forget to inform the fire brigade that highly flammable material is stored on site or they say: 'We are on fire' and hang up.

The matrix below shows the key information that should be

to hand when making an emergency call. It also shows who
else to call after you have made the initial emergency call.

	In the event of an emergency
1.	Activate alarm (this may mean pressing buttons or dialling a pre-set code in your phone system). Dial 999.
2.	Identify which service(s) you want: Fire, Police or Ambulance.
3.	Give the address of your premises: The Factory 1 The Street Anytown A1 5AB The post code can be used to identify your exact location, give it if you know it.
4.	Describe the nature of the problem – fire in warehouse storing plastics, accident in cutting room – whatever it is, give as much detail as you know. Remember the staff in the emergency call centre have already alerted the appropriate team. They are already on their way but they can summon additional resources if they have enough information.
5.	Finally who are you? Your name and your role can help to eliminate hoax calls. Also, when the appropriate service arrives you can make yourself known to the crew.

If you have business premises, this information should be
available to all staff and should, at the very least, be
displayed prominently in each working area, adjacent to a
telephone.

When the emergency service(s) arrive they should be met

and directed to the emergency. This is a separate role to that of ensuring all staff are evacuated safely, although both will report to the lead emergency services officer. This individual will almost certainly take charge of the situation from that point onwards and you and your staff should be aware of this. The incident manager will advise you what to do and when, but it is almost inevitable that once all staff are accounted for, everyone excepting essential staff will be sent home.

You may have to find petty cash to enable staff to get home, especially if they have left coats and wallets in the office. Keep a record of what you have paid to staff, if possible. Do not try to make arrangements for subsequent days at this time. Tell staff that you will contact them – another good reason for keeping staff contact lists up to date.

Calling an ambulance for an individual member of staff who has been taken ill has been included here to avoid panic-stricken calls. However, if the reason for the ambulance is an industrial accident or injury at work, there may be a need to follow your health and safety procedures and call the relevant department at the DTI.

Evacuation plans

You need to have a workable evacuation plan for your business. This means having the following:

- The means to raise the alarm
- Guidelines on when to evacuate the premises
- Instructions on how to evacuate the premises with contingency plans if normal exits are blocked

- A safe place to congregate
- A mechanism to check that everyone is accounted for
- A reporting mechanism
- A procedure for allowing a return to the building
- A procedure when a return is not possible
- Regular practices

The above list deals with the main points, but what does it mean in practical terms? If your business employs more than one or two people and you have separate business premises with more than one floor, stairs, lifts and multiple exits you will almost certainly already have an evacuation plan. Your local fire officer will have given you advice or the last occupants of the premises will have left the instructions pinned to the walls. All commercial buildings should be inspected by the local fire prevention officer and recommendations made. These may include the fitting of alarm systems that should be tested regularly.

In addition, you should also be carrying out regular evacuation drills.

If you are running your business from home or from a rented room in someone else's premises, it is unlikely that you have even thought about it. Very few families think about how to evacuate their own home although if they did, fewer would need to be rescued.

If you are planning an evacuation route, from each room find the shortest route outside using normal hallways and exits. Check that route for obstacles, if smoke is blindingly thick, the little table holding the phone directories will get in the way if it is in the direct path to the door. Remove the obstacles. Although this refers to the home office, all businesses should carry out similar checks. Discarded equipment in corridors and stairwells is not only a breach of health and safety rules, but may cost you your life in an emergency.

If you work in commercial premises, fire doors have to be fitted and all main exit doors should open outwards. This will not be the case in converted houses or in your own home. Check all doors, make sure that they open smoothly, that handles are secure and that they cannot be accidentally locked. If secure entry systems have been fitted, make sure that you and your staff know how to override them in an emergency.

Identify a place outside, well away from the building to congregate. There must be enough space for people to gather without overcrowding and without blocking public rights of way. Emergency services must not be hindered. From your home, this may be on the street outside or in the garden. Again think of hazards and obstacles en route to your chosen spot. The ornamental pond may look lovely on a bright sunny day, but it is less attractive on a dark foggy November evening when you fall in it after the vandals have set the place ablaze by pushing fireworks through the letter-box.

Write down in clear detail the route to the evacuation point from each room. In a family house make sure that everyone knows how to get out and where to go. If your working premises are separate from your home, then put evacuation notices on the wall in each room. If you work from home this may be regarded as obsessive.

From each room, office or workspace you should also identify an alternative escape route. On ground floors this is likely to be through windows, if they are of an appropriate size. On upper floors you should consider external fire escapes, or at the very least, roll-up ladders. These will be in place in commercial premises but if you are working from a spare bedroom in your house, you may wish to consider this. Jumping from upstairs windows is not a reasonable option. Again make sure that every occupant of the premises knows what the alternatives are.

Evacuation plans in smaller premises may conflict with security precautions. If smashing windows is a last resort, then an appropriate tool to do this must be provided in the vicinity.

Make sure that you practise an evacuation drill every 3–6 months, even if it is only you and your friend, it might save your life. Vary the drill by adding in make-believe hazards so that everyone learns all potential escape routes.

If you are in any doubt at all, ask your local fire prevention officer to advise you, particularly if there are disabled employees or any unusual or hazardous circumstances to consider. By practising evacuation drills regularly you will avoid panic and make sure that the instructions are clear and understood. Every second will count.

There may be items that you want to remove as you evacuate – do not even consider it. If you have prepared your business recovery plan fully, everything you need should be duplicated elsewhere and/or insured. The cat will get out and the goldfish will probably survive.

When you have evacuated the building, you need to make sure everyone is accounted for. If there are up to ten of you, you will know who is missing. If there are more of you than this, appoint fire wardens who will know their patch and how to get everyone out. The fire warden might have a luminous yellow jacket to wear, but more importantly they need an up-to-date list of all employees who must be accounted for. The fire wardens are the last people to leave the building and, if appropriate, they will ensure that all fire doors are closed.

Essential contact management

During a disaster, or in the immediate aftermath, you will not be thinking about who you need to contact. After the emergency services have arrived, the ambulance has driven down the road or customs and excise have just searched your premises and taken away your computer systems, the immediate response is to speak to your boss or your nearest and dearest, depending upon the exact situation. After that who then?

The table below is a check-list of who needs to be contacted in the relevant circumstances. If these people need to be contacted, you will need their contact details. When you make your own copy of this list do not forget to add these details to it.

Contact management table	Natural and other disasters			Criminal activity			Death or injury		Other events	
	Fire	Flood	Explosion	Fraud	Theft	Criminal Damage	Major Accident	Death	Service supply failure	
Fire service	•	•	•				•			
Police	•		•	•	•	•	•	•		
Ambulance							•	•		
Staff next of kin							•	•		
Staff members	•	•	•		•	•	•	•		
Coroner								•		
Insurers	•	•	•	•	•	•	•			
Gas supplier	•	•	•						•	
Water service provider	•	•	•						•	
Electricity supplier	•	•	•						•	
Telecommunications provider	•		•			•			•	
IT disaster specialists	•	•	•		•	•			•	
Disaster recovery specialist	•	•	•			•				
Local authority		•								
Architect	•		•							
Surveyor	•	•	•							
Glazier						•				
Builder						•				
Lawyers			•	•	•	•	•	•		
Department of Trade	•		•	•			•	•		

On Tuesday and Wednesday some of the activities you carried out were the development of contact lists for:

- Staff
- Suppliers
- Customers

You will need these lists now, because they are vital to communications about what you are going to do. If your list is short, calling may be the responsibility of just one person. In a larger organisation the list is likely to be subdivided by department. The supplier lists were set up as tables (see page 46) giving details of who to call and what to tell them or ask for. Use the contact table on page 68 to decide who to call.

Use the staff list first to make sure that everyone is accounted for at the time of the disaster and subsequently to advise your staff of what to do and where to go in the immediate future. (See section on evacuation, p. 61.)

You will use your supplier list to call your insurers and the utility companies to check supplies to your premises. Call the coroner if anyone died. Your bank and any goods suppliers need to be called to divert or postpone deliveries. Refer to your list and tick everything off as you do it. Each of your site or departmental plans should include a check-list of who to inform and what to tell them.

If suppliers give you instructions, get the name of the person you are talking to and their job title. Write down the instructions given, read them back to the person you are talking to and confirm them in writing later. Keep all the notes – if you have disputes later this may ensure that you do not pay penalties or lose insurance claims.

Your customers also need to know what is happening. If you

are a retail business, an answering machine message and a sign on the door may be sufficient. If you are a manufacturer, then customers must be advised immediately by phone of delays or cancellation to their orders. This should be followed up in writing. A service organisation's customers may suffer little impact if your staff routinely work on clients' premises. Clients should, however, still be told. Your customer list will tell you how to handle each one.

Your plan will operate smoothly if you have kept your lists up to date. If you have not you may have to rely on memory. Worse, you will not be able to delegate this task while you direct the overall recovery operation.

Media management

We live in an age where communications are instant. The video camera and digital transmission of pictures means that storm, fire and flood disasters can be front-page news and on local and national TV within minutes. Anyone with a camera to hand will take pictures. Your disaster may be seen by your customers before you have had time to assess the damage. Your clients will make assumptions about your ability to recover unless you have made appropriate preparations.

If your organisation is large enough you will have someone to handle Public Relations, but if you are a small business, responsibility for talking to the media lies with you.

Clearly in situations like fire, where you do not know how extensive the damage is until a surveyor arrives, you cannot make optimistic predictions. However, you can state that contingency plans have always been in place and that these

have been set in motion. Your customers will be informed
and you can give out an emergency contact number.

- DO NOT talk to reporters and admit that you are
  ruined (even if you are). The sound bite lasts forever.
  Remember Gerald Ratner – it cost his organisation
  their trade name and millions of pounds through one
  comment
- DO use the media to give your customers positive
  information, such as phone numbers to call,
  reassurance that deliveries are unaffected or any
  other constructive statements
- It you do not know what the situation is then say: 'It's
  too early to comment, we have contingency plans for
  these situations and we will issue a statement later'

The media might come back to you if the situation is an
ongoing one: 'Flooding continues into second week!' By this
time you should be able to give them a prepared statement,
but if you are news for only a few hours, make sure you give
out positive messages.

Having said all of this, your staff may enjoy their 15 minutes
of fame and they may make the kind of comments that you
would rather they did not. They are less likely to do this if
they have been involved in developing your recovery plan.
Many organisations also make a point of regularly reminding
their staff NOT to discuss company business with the press,
but to refer all enquiries to the relevant person. Make sure
they know who that person is.

You may find yourself in a situation where you need to give

details to the press because the incident is significant. If this is the case the following guidelines should help:

- Gather as much factual information as you can about the incident and then prepare a press statement based on that information
- Throughout the incident confine yourself to facts, do not speculate about cause, apportion blame or estimate damage
- Do not release the names of the dead or injured, unless you are certain that next of kin have been informed
- Select a suitable room (it may be an office or similar room on your premises, it may be a meeting room in a hotel or local hall) with enough space to accommodate newspaper, radio and television reporters. If space is limited and there are large numbers, restrict representation to one per channel or publication. Try to ensure that the press are kept away from members of your staff who may be distressed or are continuing to work
- Ensure that the room is supervised at all times and do not leave information lying around
- Arrange for telephone and toilet facilities and refreshments (tea or coffee) if the situation merits it
- Issue progress reports
- Only allow pictures to be taken if it is safe to do so

After the event

- The pictures that are taken by the media might be useful as part of your insurance claim. Do not hesitate to ask them for copies
- Read what is written about the event. The reports in the papers and on TV may be factually inaccurate, write to them and ask them to publish the correct information

Finally

Most news stories fade away very quickly and yours will be no exception, unless legal action of one sort or another follows it. If this is the case, think carefully about press briefings and make sure that you follow the advice of your solicitors.

Summary

Today you have dealt with a disaster in progress. In reality the events will take on a life of their own and until they have reached a conclusion – the fire is out or the dust has settled – you can only act to ensure the safety of yourself and your staff. Tomorrow we will look at how to handle the aftermath and implement your recovery plan.

Handling a disaster – what do I do next?

Implementing your recovery plan

The morning after is when depression really strikes and the enormity of the event may hit you. The sooner you start to work on recovery, the easier it is. Today we will look at how to get this process going.

- Assessing the damage
- Investigations
- Setting up the recovery team
- Calling in specialists
- Communications
- Step by step
- Keeping track and counting the cost

Assessing the damage

This section looks at specific actions that will take place during the next few hours and days. When you and your team get a chance, as early in the process as possible, you should all write down exactly what happened. Do not wait to be interviewed by assessors or fire investigators. Make notes of anything and everything that you think may be important. There are two reasons for this:

- First, your memory of the event will change over time. I have no recollection of the second train hitting my train during the Clapham train crash. The evidence shows that it did and I have no ideas why I can't remember it, but it demonstrates that it is important to write down details as soon as possible
- The second reason is to help you in the future. You know what went wrong at the time and you can think about what could have been done better. You would be very unlucky to experience an identical disaster at a later date, but your experiences will help you to reassess your future recovery plans or help another organisation improve theirs

Death and injury

There is no easy way to handle this topic and the extent to which your organisation is affected will not be known until after the event. Hopefully there will be no casualties, but if there are you will need to handle things sensitively. This must also be regarded as one of the top priorities.

- Do not disclose personal details of casualties to the press until the next of kin have been informed
- If staff have been injured, someone should visit them, either in hospital or at home, to give any reassurance that might be needed. BUT do not discuss blame or compensation at this stage
- If there are any fatalities, then a visit to the next of kin is appropriate, but be sensitive about timing. The coroner will have to be informed and someone will

almost certainly have to attend an inquest. Once again, discussions about compensation and insurance will have to wait until investigations are completed

- Tell the rest of your staff what has happened. There is no need to go into explicit detail but do not compound what is already a traumatic situation by failing to inform them yourself – if you do not the press will
- Have information about counselling organisations to hand

Starting recovery

The morning after can be too late for some recovery to be effectively carried out. If you have suffered a bomb, fire, flood accident or storm damage you should start recovery as soon as the emergency services and/or structural engineers say your premises are safe to enter.

You may have to wait for your insurance assessor before entering the premises. Make sure that you are covered for any damage that might be caused from the time the emergency services leave the site until the assessor arrives.

Your insurance company may give you very specific instructions on what you can or cannot do and you should have details of this in your plan. They may give you exact instructions when you first report the problem. You should write these instructions down and read them back to the insurance contact. Make sure that your call has a reference number and make a note of it.

However, assuming that you are allowed access to your premises, the first thing you should do is to take photographs or video footage of everything. Opportunists will steal anything worth having as soon as the site is left unattended. Sightseers can inadvertently remove or break things and further damage may be caused by exposure to the weather.

The photographs you take should be catalogued with the date and time and a description of what is being photographed. These pictures are your evidence. Do not forget to include a reference in the photograph, a scale (ruler or similar) and proof of the date or time (more difficult but possible with most video or digital cameras). The insurance assessor should do something similar. The pictures will help you in case of dispute.

Ideally you will have a security company on your list of suppliers to call, who will board up your premises and make them secure and, if necessary, provide a guard service. Your insurers will pay for this, but they will not pay for additional damage caused by looters or similar if you have made no effort to protect yourself.

When you reviewed your equipment and stock earlier in the week, you will have identified items that need to be salvaged as quickly as possible. Computer hard discs may contain recoverable data, even if the machine itself is smoke blackened and wet.

Remove all salvageable items to a secure location, catalogue and photograph them. You can relate these back to the original photographs of the site if necessary. If you have been allowed to do this before the insurance assessor attends he or she must visit this location as well in order to assess the salvage value of these items.

The next visitors to the site are likely to be investigators, particularly if you have suffered fire, bomb or accident damage. If serious crime is suspected, the premises will be sealed by the police as soon as the fire crews and structural specialists leave the site. They will search for evidence and only when they have finished their investigation will you be able to begin the process of rebuilding.

Your surveyors and the insurance assessor will give you an idea of what needs to be done and the likely cost. The fate of your site will depend on your decision of what to do in your business recovery plan.

Investigations

Under certain circumstances, investigations will be carried out to determine why your disaster happened and who was responsible. In almost all cases your insurers will carry out some investigations to establish cause. The exceptions are natural disasters like earthquake or flood.

- *Negligence*: Accidents such as chemical spills and explosions will be investigated by fire officers and the health and safety officers in the Department of Trade and Industry. Their aim is to ensure that your company did not bring the accident about through negligence. If negligence is proven you may find yourself facing legal actions for compensation, as well as losing rights to insurance payments.

- *Criminal damage*: The police will investigate any disasters brought about by criminal damage.

- *Terrorist activity*: The police and possibly special branch will investigate terrorist activity. If your business is politically sensitive you should take extra precautions to protect yourself and your staff. You should also be prepared to check the background of new employees.

- *Fraud*: If the insurance company suspects fraud, they will investigate the financial health of the company and its owners. If you have not taken steps to protect your financial information you may find it more difficult to prove that you are not trying to pull a fast one.

- *The coroner*: If anyone dies as a result of the disaster the coroner has to be informed and an inquest held. The verdict of the coroner will be appropriate to the reason behind the disaster. Accidents are just that, but if any criminal activity is suspected an open verdict will be given. If criminal activity is proven the verdict will be murder or manslaughter.

If negligence by you or your employees is proven you could be sued.

Setting up the recovery team

In your plan you have identified key individuals who will help you recover. Call these people first and meet to agree the action plan. If your premises are unusable you will have to start working on the alternatives. The first of these is where are you going to meet. This should be in your plan, but if it is not or, for some reason, it is unavailable you have the following options:

> - Your home if it is convenient to your site
> - A local hotel or hall – the latter can often be rented quite cheaply for a few hours, but you may find yourself competing with the local toddler group or WI
> - A spare office or meeting room in another organisation – this might be a reciprocal arrangement you have made with another business
> - Rented office accommodation or business space – this may be part of your recovery plan or you may be able to find available space at short notice locally

All of the options suggested have advantages and disadvantages but the important thing is to meet and get started. You will also need your emergency pack and copies of the plan.

As soon as your team members have got together, go through the plans for each of them quickly and confirm what

needs to be done. Your plan was built on the basis of a best guess. You now know exactly what situation you find yourself in and you should revise the activities accordingly. Make sure that everyone amends their copy of the plan, with the relevant changes. Prioritise all of the activities. It is pointless arranging for stand-by equipment to be delivered, until you are sure that the alternative premises are accessible. Agree a meeting for feedback. Schedule and make sure that everyone attends all meetings – it may seem to be going smoothly, but unless you discuss progress, minor glitches can turn into major handicaps.

Keep control of the spend. You know what you need and you will have a good idea of what you can afford to spend, but you do not need each team member to go and buy the same items when, with a bit of forethought, they can be shared or borrowed.

Most of this stage relies on the plans and the lists you have made. Inevitably something will have been forgotten – this need not be a problem, just discuss it with your team and seek ideas. If your planning was thorough there will be no show-stoppers.

Calling in specialists

This will test the organisations that you have chosen to help you. You should have rehearsed your requirements with them – particularly important in respect of resuming IT systems. Once again, you will have agreed in advance what needs to be done, but circumstances may change as a result of the disaster. Go over the agreement and modify it if necessary. Such modifications should only be minor. Contractually your specialists should deliver what they agreed to deliver within an agreed period of time. Do not forget to give them the agreed notice period. You may have an agreement that systems will be up and running within 48 hours of notification. Make sure that this is scheduled into your plan and if it is going to take you longer than the agreed notice period to get a site ready for the specialists, then let them know. Someone must coordinate all activities.

The best laid plans can go awry. If your disaster is the result of an even bigger catastrophe affecting a large area, for example, unprecedented flooding, then you may have to significantly revise your plans. There is no easy preparation for this, especially if the specialists you have called in are also facing an unprecedented workload.

Communications

Communication needs to be maintained. If your disaster is of public interest, you should make sure that any information given to the press is accurate and positive. Your staff will need reassurance on a regular basis, particularly if they are waiting to hear when to return to work. Your customers will be reassured if you can give them positive news, but do not shrink from giving them bad news. They are more likely to stick with you if they know what is going on. Your suppliers are only too keen to help you so let them know what they can do – not many businesses can afford to lose customers.

At each feedback meeting decide whether or not to pass information on to others. Agree on what you will say and recognise that conflicting information is damaging.

Step by step

Cashflow takes priority here. Your insurers will pay out, but not until they are satisfied with your claim. Make sure you claim promptly and supply the insurers with all of the relevant information. Talk to your bank – they will lend you money to keep going provided that you have a plan. You should have made these arrangements before the disaster occurred.

Accommodation

The first thing to tackle is accommodation. If your own premises are unusable you should now be calling up the alternatives in your support list. Appropriate premises need to be opened up and prepared for business. You may have a hot site as an interim arrangement but you may prefer to set up a more permanent location, especially if significant rebuilding works are necessary. If only part of your site is damaged then the sooner repairs can start the better. Get the estimates, confirm that the insurer will pay and then get started.

Staff

Your staff will need to be contacted. Contact them at home by phone and follow up with a letter, advising them when and where to report to work. Your recovery team will work with you on a daily basis to keep your business going and they will know what they have to do. Communication is very important. If there were deaths or injuries as a result of the disaster, staff need time to grieve. You may need to seek counselling services for staff and they will certainly need reassurance about their jobs. You cannot stop paying them, although if you believe that you will have to stop trading then you can pay them wages in lieu of notice.

A reduction in the numbers of staff may be necessary to survive the crisis, but think this through carefully. If you expect to be back to full capacity quickly, discuss the options open to you with your staff. They may prefer to work fewer hours for a short period and some may choose to leave with the option to return in 3 or 6 months. Communication is critical.

Equipment

Salvage what you can or organise replacements. Earlier we looked at the availability of specialist tools. If you are forced to wait for the new equipment, you may prefer to use the time for some research and development. You have nothing to lose by some experimentation or investigation of other methods. It is important not to waste opportunities. If staff cannot work until the equipment arrives, is it practical to invest in training? Cross-skilling or the learning of new skills may ensure that if you are forced to move on with a reduced workforce, they are fully trained for the job.

Suppliers

Hopefully you have put emergency plans in place with your suppliers and all you have to do is call them to advise them of what to deliver and to where. Your suppliers need to be reassured that you will be able to pay for your orders. Loss of supplies already on site should be covered by insurance. Extra supplies will be covered by sales eventually, but in the interim you may have to pay for supplies out of cash in the bank.

Customers

Notify your customers promptly if there are going to be delays to deliveries. Let then know what has happened, but reassure them. Tell them what you are doing to ensure continuity of supply or service. As part of your business you should have a facility to send letters to all of your customers – you may have to retain enough headed paper in your emergency pack to do this, but do it promptly. Silence will make your customers believe that you are struggling and they may take their business elsewhere. Remember you are not the only one who has alternative suppliers.

If you are going to cease trading, write and let your customers know, but not before you have sold your client list to one of your competitors. Whatever the outcome do not forget to thank them for their support.

Keeping track

Part of the problem after a disaster is understanding everything that is going on. If you have a good plan, your business will continue, albeit on different premises or by manoeuvring things around. Everyone still has their job to do but, in addition, someone has to take control of repairs and recovery, manage the finances, deal with the insurance claims, give evidence to investigations, ensure that all the staff are happy and communicate with suppliers and customers. This is a heavy load to bear. It is also very stressful.

The trick is in the planning. If you have put together a reasonable recovery plan, there will be a short lull in activity while all the various strands are being pulled together. Use this time to make a plan of action for the future. There will be a number of headings to work under:

Insurance
This is the obvious one and it has several subheadings:

- *Making a claim*: Identify what you need to claim against for each policy that you hold. Complete the relevant forms, supplying the appropriate evidence (assessors reports, photographs, receipts, investigation reports). Keep copies of everything and put details of who has received what in a diary (buy one, draw one up or keep a computerised record of every transaction that takes place, whether it is a letter, telephone call or fax). Your claim is unlikely to be simple so make sure that you keep a record of everything.

- *Payment of Claim*: The claim has been agreed and a cheque has arrived. Make sure that cash is assigned to the appropriate part of the business. For accounting purposes, you should have set up a separate set of expense codes to cope with the additional costs incurred by the disaster. Unless you are a very small business, you will need to track how costs were accrued and funded, whether from insurance claims or operating profits. If the disaster you have suffered is likely to put you out of business, it is even more important to track your income and expenditure because you will almost certainly want to maximise the former and minimise the latter. If you have an accountant, decide with them the best way to manage your finanacial situation.

Rebuilding

This often cannot start until investigations are complete and insurance claims are agreed. You may not be able to clear the site until this is done. Total destruction is the easiest to handle because when the site is cleared of rubble, rebuilding can begin. If the site is rented or leased, there may be shared insurance claims. If you own the site you might decide to operate from alternative premises and rebuild. You may prefer to continue operating from a new site and sell the old site for redevelopment.

If only part of the building has been damaged and overall it is structurally sound you will probably be allowed to start rebuilding work quite quickly. However, bear in mind the following. Was there anything about the building that made it particularly vulnerable to the disaster you suffered – if so can you modify the building to compensate in future? Is there anything that you want to change now that you have the opportunity. You may have to add additional capital to the rebuilding, but if it improves the business it is worth investing. Do not forget to apply for the appropriate planning permission before making changes. Your local authority will let you know what other permissions you need in respect of demolition, change of use and rebuilding.

Compensation claims
Litigation is commonplace and the following types of claim may be made against you or by you:

- Your employees may sue you for injury and damages or you might sue a supplier for injury or damages

- The owner of the building or site may sue you for damages or you might sue them for negligence

- Your customers and suppliers may sue you for breach of contract

Inevitably there will be claims of one sort or another and these have to be handled by a competent lawyer. You need to all have the evidence to hand. Ensure that you have copies of everything – doctors' reports, medical reports and investigators' reports will all need to be collated. Your insurance company may cover the costs under third-party liability insurance, but do not sign off claims against you until you are sure that everything has been accounted for.

Counting the cost

If you have managed your income and expenditure throughout this period, it will be relatively easy to identify the financial cost of the disaster. However, this is not the only price that you and your organisation will pay.

The long-term effects of stress can be damaging and may appear some considerable time after the event. Do not be surprised if you or members of staff become depressed at a time when everything has got better. Be prepared for increased absence due to minor illnesses. You may find that staff turnover also increases for a while. These are the uncounted costs of a disaster. If the damage you have experienced relates to theft or fraud, confidence in your company could dip. It takes a while for trust to be recovered.

Summary

Friday has been spent communicating and organising. All the preparation you have done in the preceding days has been put to use. You will have spent many hours talking to suppliers, customers and staff. Your staff, if they are aware of the business recovery plan will have been invaluable in helping you to carry out the many tasks you have to do. You will also have spent a lot of time handling investigations and claims. Your business is unique – the event it has suffered may have many things in common with other disasters that strike other businesses but they all have aspects that apply to them alone. How you emerge from this cannot be predicted although planning will contribute significantly to survival.

Review

The last day is a day of reflection. What worked? What did not and why? It is also a day for reiteration – your business is not a static environment and you need to keep pace with change. Last but not least, if after reading this book you want someone else to help you put this plan together, who should you go to?

- Back to normal
- The end of the road
- Did it work?
- Keeping it up to date
- Where to get more help

Back to normal

When you find yourself working normally from new or
newly rebuilt or refurbished premises, you can probably
assume that things are back to normal. However, you should
not close the book here. Today will give you the opportunity
to review what happened and remind you to revise the plan
in the light of both experience and the changes you have
made. You should take the time to congratulate yourself and
your staff or partners on a job well done. Have a party to
celebrate your success and remember to thank everybody
who contributed to your recovery.

The end of the road

The hardest of all outcomes is when, despite your best efforts,
the disaster has ruined your business. Insurance should see to
it that you emerge financially solvent but it may be that the
damage was simply too great, everything took too long or, for
personal reasons, it is too difficult to continue.

Deciding to wind up the business is not an easy option
because it is not realistic to walk away. You will have to carry
out some activities to close the business down and you
should use this opportunity to maximise your options.

What have you got that is of value to others?

- A site. Even if it is derelict it may be worth investigating
  the planning options. Sites with some of the
  bureaucracy taken care of are likely to be worth more
- Your customer/client list. Whatever your business,
  your customers will need an alternative supplier.

> Contact your competitors and sell your client details to them
> - Stock and equipment will usually raise more if sold privately, so try to do this if you can. Make sure that insurance companies do not have a prior claim
> - Your staff are more likely to be employed by competitors if they come with good references and outstanding orders from clients

You may of course be able to sell the business in its entirety, despite damage, to a competitor. This can be a long process, so be prepared for this and decide what your trading strategy will be.

Did it work?

Reviewing how well your plan worked is not something you will think of immediately. Should you find yourself in the position of rewriting your plan after a recovery situation, then it is probably fair to spend a little time on identifying what did and did not work and revising your thinking accordingly. Many recovery plans are never tested in anger and many disaster recovery planners have never worked through a disaster. Share your experience at your local business forum or at appropriate business seminars. You may gain helpful insights from others who have faced disastrous experiences.

Most people who have encountered a disaster situation will say something like: 'I never realised how much dust there would be' or, 'I didn't know smoke was so thick', or 'that flooded rooms could smell so bad'. All of these insights should encourage you to make sure that:

Do test your plan if you can, it will be informative even if the situation is a make-believe one.

- You put dust masks in your emergency pack
- Your emergency lighting is bright and situated in appropriate places
- You ensure that your clean up plans take account of sewage disposal

Keeping it up to date

No apology is made for repeating this. Your plan needs to be kept under review and it should be updated at least every 3 months. This may seem unduly onerous, but if you maintain your plan electronically updates should only take a few minutes. Every project you undertake should contain a section on disaster recovery. This will contribute to the plan, ensuring that it adapts with your organisation. If you undergo a major restructure or merge with another company, sorting out the business recovery plan should be one of the earliest activities. You will be at your most vulnerable at such a time.

Where to get more help

For some of you, this section of the book will be the most useful. It contains names, addresses and contact numbers of organisations who can assist you with preparing your plan.

The internet will be the first port of call for many of you because the search engines can identify almost anything you want in respect of business recovery planning. The only problem is refining your search so that it is relevant to you and your organisation.

Your local library will also hold various directories that contain the names and addresses of local organisations that will be able to provide some of the services you need.

Consultants

There are many organisations that offer business recovery planning consultancy. If you decide that you want to use a specialist service you can expect to pay anything from £300–£1500 a day. BUT you do not necessarily get what you pay for. The consultant should not actually do very many days' work. The biggest success factor with business recovery planning is for you and your colleagues to understand what the plan is and how it will work. A consultant can guide you through this process but they should not write your plan for you.

You must own your plan so if you choose to ask someone to help you this is what they should do:

- *Identify risks*: this means looking at your business, its location and processes.

- *Identify key systems*: define what your business does.

- *Identify key employees*: look at who is important.

Your consultant should then work with you and your team to document all of this in a similar way to the activities described in this book. They will facilitate meetings and ask you to deliver appropriate information such as insurance policies, held and so on. They may document findings, but the contributors will be you and your staff. The discussion process is important. If that does not happen, how will you know what everything means?

The consultant may identify suppliers of specific services for you, gathering costs and possibly making recommendations, but again you should be in control and decide what to use and what not to. The plan, when complete should be presented to you for confirmation. Its content should hold no surprises for you.

Alternatively you can prepare your own plan, as described, and then ask a specialist to validate it. This is a much less expensive option and all that is left for you do is to fill in any gaps that the consultant identifies.

Tools
There is software available that takes you through the analysis process in a similar way to this book. You will fill in charts and tables according to your organisation structure. The end result will be a plan – one person could complete all the information, although it is intended that the various templates are completed by different members of the organisation. The software costs about £400 and some insurance brokers will offer the software as part of the package for business recovery policies. The software is well developed and has stood the test of time. The weakness in using the software lies with those tasked with putting the plan together, if they fail to communicate what they are doing to the rest of their organisation. Like any plan it will only be of any use if the right people know about it. A well

known supplier of such software is the Disaster Recovery
Specialist

Ark & General
Walker's Rise, Hednesford
Staffs, WS12 5QU
Tel 01543 878364   main@arkgen.co.uk

If you decide that you would still like help from a consultant
you can contact me:

Jacqueline Chapman
Westfield House, 11 Gidding Road,
Sawtry, Cambs.
PE28 5TS

Tel: 01487 832941
E-mail: Jacquiechapman@aol.com

Service organisations
There are a number of organisations besides the emergency
services, that can help you should disaster occur. The
simplest way to find details in your local area is to look in the
Yellow Pages or on the internet.

• *Department of Trade & Industry*: will provide information
  about the various regulations relating to business disasters
  or accidents.

  DTI HQ
  1 Victoria Street
  London
  SW1H 0ET
  Tel: 020 7215 5000
  Website: www.dti.gov.uk

- *Disaster recovery specialists*: your insurance company will recommend someone. Find out about them before you need to use them.

- *Fire protection services*: the fire safety officer from your local fire station will advise you what you need to do, but the equipment (alarms, fire fighting equipment and fire escapes) may be obtained from a commercial supplier. Some of these will include advice on fire safety and evacuation plans.

- *Flood damage*: the environment agency will give flood warnings. Their general enquiry line offers some advice and assistance.

  The Environment Agency
  Rio House, Waterside Drive,
  Aztec West, Almondsbury,
  Bristol BS32 4UD
  Floodline: 0845 988 1188
  General Enquiries: 0845 933 3111

- *Health and Safety*: whatever your business uses in the course of its operations, you are legally bound by the regulations issued by the Health & Safety Executive. Details of your commitment can be found on their website www.hse.gov.uk or you can call their main office on 01256 404000 or 01245 706200.

- *Insurance brokers*: most commercial insurance can only be obtained through a broker. The British Insurance Brokers Association (BIBA) will advise you of members in your area, call 020 7623 9043.

- *Investigators*: theft and fraud can decimate your business, particularly if it is carried out by employees. If you are at risk in this respect you may choose to employ a private investigator.

- *Security services*: alarms, guards and patrols equipment may all be necessary to protect your business. Your local crime prevention officer should be your first port of call. He or she will be aware of the companies in your area that specialise in protective security.

- *Locksmiths*: most locksmiths offer 24-hour services that not only cater for replacing or opening damaged locks, but also for emergency repairs to vandalised or theft damaged premises. Many are members of the Master Locksmiths Association.

- *Salvage:* your insurance company should advise you on salvage experts because they will have commercial relationships with preferred suppliers.